W9-BOC-923

HOME RUN!

SCIENCE PROJECTS

with BASEBALL

and SOFTBALL

SPORTS SCIENCE PROJECTS
SCORE!

GOAL!
SCIENCE PROJECTS
with SOCCER

ISBN-13: 978-0-7660-3106-7
ISBN-10:　　0-7660-3106-3

HOME RUN!
SCIENCE PROJECTS
with BASEBALL and SOFTBALL

ISBN-13: 978-0-7660-3365-8
ISBN-10:　　0-7660-3365-1

SLAM DUNK!
SCIENCE PROJECTS
with BASKETBALL

ISBN-13: 978-0-7660-3366-5
ISBN-10:　　0-7660-3366-X

WHEELS!
SCIENCE PROJECTS
with BICYCLES, SKATEBOARDS and SKATES

ISBN-13: 978-0-7660-3107-4
ISBN-10:　　0-7660-3107-1

HOME RUN!

SCIENCE PROJECTS
with BASEBALL
and SOFTBALL

Robert L. Bonnet and Dan Keen

 Enslow Publishers, Inc.
40 Industrial Road
Box 398
Berkeley Heights, NJ 07922
USA
http://www.enslow.com

*For my daughter-in-law, Susan Bonnet, who has been a fine wife
to my son and a great mother to their children—R.L.B.*

For my granddaughter, Sarah Gummel—D.K.

Library of Congress Cataloging-in-Publication Data

Bonnet, Robert L.
    Home run! : science projects with baseball and softball / Robert L. Bonnet and Dan Keen.
        p. cm. — (Score! Sports science projects)
    Includes bibliographical references and index.
    Summary: "Provides several science experiments using physics and baseball or softball"—Provided by publisher.
    ISBN-13: 978-0-7660-3365-8
    1. Physics—Experiments—Juvenile literature. 2. Baseball—Experiments—Juvenile literature. 3. Softball—Experiments—Juvenile literature. 4. Motion—Experiments—Juvenile literature. 5. Force and energy—Experiments—Juvenile literature. 6. Science projects—Juvenile literature. I. Keen, Dan. II. Title.
    QC26.B65 2009
    530.078—dc22   2008003005

ISBN-10: 0-7660-3365-1

Printed in the United States of America

10 9 8 7 6 5 4 3 2 1

To Our Readers: We have done our best to make sure all Internet Addresses in this book were active and appropriate when we went to press. However, the author and the publisher have no control over and assume no liability for the material available on those Internet sites or on other Web sites they may link to. Any comments or suggestions can be sent by e-mail to comments@enslow.com or to the address on the back cover.

Every effort has been made to locate all copyright holders of material used in this book. If any errors or omissions have occurred, corrections will be made in future editions of this book.

♻ Enslow Publishers, Inc., is committed to printing our books on recycled paper. The paper in every book contains 10% to 30% post-consumer waste (PCW). The cover board on the outside of each book contains 100% PCW. Our goal is to do our part to help young people and the environment too!

Illustration Credits: All illustrations by Stephen F. Delisle, except Robert Gummel, p. 10.

Photo Credits: All photos by Shutterstock, except Library of Congress, Prints & Photographs Division, p. 66.

Cover Illustration: Shutterstock

CONTENTS

🔻 Indicates experiments that are followed by Science Project Ideas.

INTRDUCTION

GET READY TO HAVE SOME FUN! IT'S TIME TO combine your love for baseball or softball with the exciting exploration of science and the world around you. Have you ever wondered how wind affects the flight of a ball? Or why runners wear cleats? This book will introduce you to the complexities of the game while teaching you some basic concepts in the fascinating science of physics.

The Scientific Method

Scientific investigations usually follow a step-by-step process to find answers to a hypothesis. A hypothesis is a statement you make based on an educated guess. The step-by-step process you take to find out if the hypothesis is true or not is called the scientific method. Let's look at an example.

Suppose you believe that hitting a baseball or softball at its center will cause it to travel farther than if it is hit off-center, near its top as it flies. This is your hypothesis. Next, you set up an experiment to test this hypothesis. You collect information (data) from your experiment. Finally, you reach a conclusion about your hypothesis based on the results you have gathered.

Remember that the goal of a science project is to find out whether your hypothesis is true or not. It doesn't matter if your experiment proves the hypothesis is not true. A successful science experiment only needs to prove or disprove the hypothesis. The famous inventor Thomas Edison tried over 1,000 different materials to find one that worked best as a filament in his lightbulb. He said, "I failed my way to success." With each material he tried that was a failure, he learned something. He found out that a particular material could be eliminated as a possible filament. He kept detailed notes so that he would not try the same material twice. If your experiment proves your hypothesis to be incorrect, your project is still a success.

Safety First

When doing any science project, safety must be the first concern.

- Carefully think through each project before beginning.
- **Have an adult present** as you do your project.
- Always wear a batting helmet when doing projects where a ball is pitched to you as a batter.
- Before swinging a bat, be sure the area is clear.

- Wear eye protection and closed-toe shoes (rather than sandals), and tie back long hair.

- Don't eat or drink while doing experiments, and never taste substances being used (unless instructed to do so).

- When doing these experiments, use only nonmercury thermometers, such as those filled with alcohol. The liquid in some thermometers is mercury. It is dangerous to breathe mercury vapor. If you have mercury thermometers, **ask an adult** to take them to a local mercury thermometer exchange location.

- Do only those experiments that are described in the book or those that have been approved by **an adult**.

- Never engage in horseplay or play practical jokes.

- Before beginning, read through the entire experimental procedure to make sure you understand all instructions, and clear all extra items from your work space.

A rain delay at a Los Angeles Angels game in Anaheim, California, had the ground crew working to cover the field.

ENVIRONMENTAL FACTORS

S ome sports, such as football, are played regardless of the weather. Despite high winds, rain, mud, sleet, or snow, the football game goes on! Weather is an important factor in playing ball, and can affect the outcome of a ball game.

Baseball and softball games, however, are stopped when it begins to rain hard. The field gets covered with tarps to keep it as dry as possible. Still, the ball field can get wet when rain begins, and the game may still be played. How does a wet field affect the game?

Wind can be a factor in how a ball travels through the air. The design, shape, and location of stadiums can affect wind currents inside them. Wind can be constant or can occur in strong, brief gusts. At Candlestick Park in San Francisco in 1961, Giants pitcher Stu Miller was actually blown off the pitcher's mound by a strong gust of wind!

Even though baseballs and softballs are fairly solid objects, they can be affected by the wind. You may have watched a professional ball game on television and seen times when the commentator remarked that if it hadn't been for the strong wind, the ball would have traveled out of the stadium for a home run.

Some modern stadiums are enclosed, but playing baseball or softball indoors does not necessarily eliminate all environmental factors. In 1965 the New York Mets accused the groundskeepers at the Houston Astrodome of manipulating the air-conditioning system. Air currents would hinder the fly balls of visiting teams while helping those hit by the Houston Astros, the home team.

Temperature also has a slight effect on the bounciness of baseballs and softballs—they have less bounce as temperature decreases. Even humidity (the amount of water in air) affects the flight of a ball through the air. The humidity can make the air more or less dense on any given day.

Let's take a look at some weather factors and their effects on a ball's movement.

EXPERIMENT **1.1**

How Does Wind Affect a Ball?

MATERIALS

- oak tag or poster board (about 28 inches by 22 inches)
- table
- two 12-ounce cans of soda (or two cans of soup)
- empty paper towel roll (the diameter of the paper towel roll must be large enough to allow a Ping-Pong ball to roll easily through it)
- adhesive tape
- hair dryer that has a low, cool setting
- several heavy books (encyclopedias work well)
- Ping-Pong ball
- pencil
- a partner

In this experiment, a rolling ball will pass by a stream of moving air to see how the air affects the path of the ball. This airstream will simulate a gust of wind or a day when winds in an outdoor stadium are strong. Make a hypothesis about how the ball's course will be affected by a gust of air that is moving sideways (laterally) to the motion of the ball.

To test your hypothesis, a comparison will be made. First, the path of a rolling ball will be plotted. Then the path will be plotted for the same ball rolling past a stream of moving air hitting it at a 90-degree angle to the path of its travel. The two paths can be compared to see if there is a difference, and if so, how much of a difference.

1 Lay a large piece of oak tag or poster board on a smooth tabletop. At one end of the poster board, stand two unopened soda cans touching each other, as shown in Figure 1. Lay one end of an empty paper towel roll on top of and between the two cans so that the cans keep it from moving side to side. The other end of the paper towel roll will rest on the poster board, making a ramp. Tape the opening of the paper towel roll to the poster board to keep it secure.

2 Place a hair dryer on the table, with its nozzle at a 90-degree angle to the paper towel roll. The hair dryer should be placed several inches away from the bottom of the paper towel roll and to the side of it. Keep the hair dryer from moving by placing several heavy books on each side of it.

3 For the first run, do not turn the hair dryer on. Have a

FIGURE 1.
How does moving air affect the path of a moving object?

partner place a Ping-Pong ball in the top opening of the paper towel roll and let it roll down the ramp. Be sure not to push the Ping-Pong ball. Just let go of it so that only the force of gravity acts on the ball. The force of gravity is constant. This will ensure that the ball will be going the same speed every time it rolls down the ramp.

4 With a pencil, make a mark on the poster board at the position where the ball rolls off the end of the board. Repeat this two more times. Label the marks A.

5 Now turn the hair dryer on a low, cool setting to blow a steady stream of air across the path of the ball. Release the ball and mark the position where the ball rolls off the end of the board. Repeat this two more times. Label these marks B.

Compare the paths of the ball with no wind (A) to those with the hair dryer turned on (B). How did the "wind" affect the path of the ball?

From this experiment, you can see that it is important for fielders to be aware of wind conditions. A strong wind at an outfielder's back will cause a fly ball to drop quicker. A strong wind blowing sideways across the field will cause a fly ball to drift to one side. A ball hit high into the air might look like it is coming straight toward a fielder, but as it descends it may change its course due to the wind. A ballplayer who knows which way the wind is blowing is better prepared to catch such a ball.

Repeat the experiment with the hair dryer blowing a stream of air at a 45-degree angle to the ball's straight path. How does the angle of the wind affect the ball's path?

SCIENCE PROJECT IDEA

If the ball travels faster, is it affected more or less by the wind? Increase the speed of the Ping-Pong ball as it exits the paper towel roll by making the paper towel ramp steeper. Measure the angle of the paper-towel ramp to the tabletop with a protractor. Keep the hair dryer on the same speed setting, and drop the ball down the ramp. Does the stream of air have a different effect on a ball that is traveling faster as it passes through a gust of air? What is the effect on the ball if the angle of the ramp is less steep?

EXPERIMENT **1.2**

Does Rain Affect a Ball's Bounce?

MATERIALS

- **an adult**
- tall stepladder
- smooth, level concrete surface (a garage floor or driveway)
- yardstick or meterstick
- marking pen
- poster board (about 28 inches by 22 inches)
- adhesive tape
- a baseball or softball
- pencil and notebook
- spray bottle containing water
- small bucket of water

A baseball or softball game may continue to be played if there is only a light rain or if it appears as though the rain will end soon. Before a game is called off due to rain, the ball and the playing field may get pretty wet. Make a hypothesis about whether the bounce of a baseball or softball will change when the ball gets wet. A change in the ball's bounce could affect the distance a batter hits the ball.

To test your hypothesis, a baseball or softball will be dropped from the same height each time onto a hard surface, simulating how a ball might hit a hard bat. The ball will be dry for the first set of three drops. Then it will have a little water sprayed on it for the second set of drops. Finally, the ball will be soaked in water for the third set. The same ball will be used instead of using separate balls to eliminate any variables there may be among balls.

1 Place a tall stepladder on a smooth, flat concrete surface, such as a garage floor or a level driveway. Using a yardstick or meterstick and a dark marking pen, make marks on a sheet of poster board every inch, or 2.5 centimeters, and write a number next to it. Attach the poster board to the side of the ladder using adhesive tape. One side of the poster board should be resting on the concrete, with the marks going up from the ground. This will be used as a reference to see how high the ball bounces each time it is dropped.

2 Have an adult stand on the stepladder and hold a dry ball (see Figure 2). Have the adult drop the ball three times. Each time it must be dropped from the exact same height. After the bounce, use your eye to line up the top (or bottom) of the ball to the lines on the poster board at the ball's highest point. Record the height of each drop in your notebook. Find the average height for each of the three

In the summer it can get too hot in Texas to play or even watch a baseball game. The Astrodome in Houston, Texas, was built so that baseball games could be played indoors in the comfort of air-conditioning. Engineers claimed to have been able to make it snow inside the Astrodome because of its tremendous air conditioning capacity!

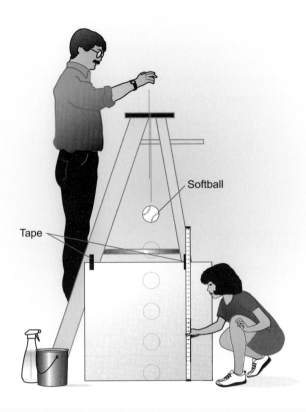

FIGURE 2.
How high a ball bounces when it is wet or dry and dropped on a hard surface gives an indication of how it may react when wet or dry and hit with a hard baseball bat.

drops. The average is found by adding the three numbers together and dividing the total by three.

3 Using a spray bottle, spritz a little water on the ball so that it is evenly moist all around, but not dripping wet. **Have the adult** drop the ball three times, and record the height of the three bounces. Calculate the average height of the bounce.

4 Place the ball in a bucket of water for several minutes so that it becomes thoroughly soaked. **Have the adult** drop it three more times. Soak the ball again before each drop. Record the bounce heights and calculate the average.

Compare the averages of the three ball conditions. Did the soaked ball bounce differently than the dry ball?

SCIENCE PROJECT IDEA

Does a baseball float? Does a softball float? If so, for how long? Weigh a dry ball, and then weigh it wet. Is a wet ball heavier? How about a wet ball that has been placed in the freezer? Compare the bounce of a dry ball to one that has been soaked in water and then frozen.

EXPERIMENT **1.3**

How Does a Wet Ball Field Affect the Movement of a Ground Ball?

MATERIALS
- **an adult**
- two 2-by-4 pieces of lumber, 8 feet long
- several 3-inch coarse-thread wood screws
- screw gun
- level grassy area
- tall stepladder
- two bricks (optional)
- baseball or softball
- tape measure or meterstick
- garden hose and water source (or buckets of water)

You may have seen a video clip on one of TV's "blooper shows" of a professional ball game where the sprinkler system mistakenly comes on in the middle of a game, drenching the players and the field. The rest of the game was played on the wet field.

Does a ground ball travel differently on wet grass than it does on dry grass? Although ball games are not played in heavy rain, games may be played in a light rain that could significantly wet the playing field. Knowing whether or not a wet playing field will affect the movement of a ground ball would be helpful to fielders. Make a hypothesis as to whether a ground ball will behave differently on a wet playing field than on a dry field.

1 Place two pieces of 2-by-4 wood, each 8 feet long, next to each other at a 90-degree angle to each other, lengthwise, as shown in Figure 3a. **Have an adult** help you attach them together using several 3-inch wood screws. The boards will be used as a ramp for launching a ball along the ground. When tilted to the side, the wood ramp will form a V, or channel, down which a ball can be rolled.

2 On a grassy lawn, set up a tall stepladder. Place one end of the ramp on a step on the ladder four or five feet off the ground. Tilt the ramp slightly so that it forms a V. To keep it in that position you can push it to one side of the step so that it rests against the vertical frame of the ladder. You could also place a brick on the ladder's step on either side of the ramp.

3 Hold a baseball or softball at the end of the ramp on the

Water can influence a ball game in many ways. If the base paths are soaked, players who try to steal bases can't get a good jump start. When they are starting to run from a stopped position, they push into softened, wet ground.

Also, if the dirt in front of home plate is wet, bunted balls will quickly stop. Hall of Fame baseball player Ty Cobb used this trick in Detroit (to keep his bunts in fair territory), and the area in front of home plate became known as Cobb's Lake.

3a

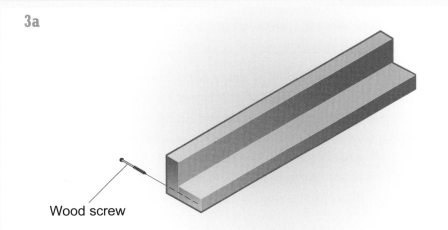

Wood screw

3b

FIGURE 3.

a. Two lengths of wood can be screwed together so that when they are turned to form a V they create a channel that can be used as a ramp for giving constant speed to a baseball or softball.

b. Compare the distances a ball travels on dry grass and wet grass.

stepladder and let go (Figure 3b). Be careful not to push the ball. The constant force of gravity must be the only force moving the ball.

4 When the ball stops rolling, use a tape measure to find the distance from the end of the ramp to the ball. Write down the distance the ball traveled along the ground. Do this three times, and then calculate the average distance. Convert all your distance measurements to the same units, such as inches or centimeters. The average is found by adding the three distances together and dividing by 3.

5 Next, using a garden hose connected to a water source (or several buckets of water), thoroughly soak the lawn area from the bottom of the ramp to several feet beyond where the ball previously stopped.

6 Drop the ball down the ramp again. Measure the distance the ball travels. Do this three times and calculate the average distance. Compare the average distances of the ball traveling on dry grass and the ball traveling on wet grass. Is there a significant difference? If so, what is the percentage of one to the other? (Percent is calculated by dividing one distance by the other and multiplying the result by 100.) Is the difference significant enough that the fielder would have to move his whole body to a new position in order to get to the ball quickly?

SCIENCE PROJECT IDEAS

- If you used a baseball for the project, repeat the experiment using a softball. If you used a softball for the project, repeat the experiment using a baseball. Are the results of the two different balls similar?

- Since there is a lot of dirt in front of home plate, along the baselines, and around the infield, repeat the experiment on dirt rather than on grass. Does wet dirt affect the movement of the ball as much as wet grass does?

- Is the height of the grass a factor? On professional ball fields, is the outfield grass cut as short as infield grass?

TRANSFER OF ENERGY

The pitcher throws the ball hard and fast. The batter swings his bat as hard as he can, accelerating the bat. There's a collision! The batter uses his arms and hands to apply a strong force to the bat. He must transfer the kinetic energy from the moving bat to the ball, and try to send that ball "outta here"!

Transfer of energy and *kinetic energy* are common terms in physics used to describe what happens in collisions. Kinetic energy is the energy an object has when it is in motion. Kinetic energy depends on the object's speed and mass. The mass of an object is the amount of material in the object. Imagine a billiard ball sitting on a pool table, and a rolling billiard ball smacking into it. Both balls have about the same mass. The rolling ball has kinetic energy. A lot of that energy is transferred to the sitting ball when the two collide, and the sitting ball starts to roll. This causes a loss of kinetic energy in the initial rolling ball. Its forward motion slows or stops.

EXPERIMENT **2.1**

How Does the Weight of a Bat Affect a Hit?

MATERIALS
- **an adult**
- a shoe box or other small cardboard box
- a stool
- several empty plastic 2-liter soda bottles
- wooden baseball or softball bat
- tape measure
- plastic bat (such as a Wiffle Ball bat)
- wooden handle from an old broom (about 1.2 meters long)
- hand saw (if necessary)
- a field

Baseball and softball bats are available in different weights. If a bat weighs less, you can swing it faster. But does that mean you could hit the ball farther with it? Is more energy transferred from the bat to the ball with a heavier, slower-moving bat than a lighter, faster-moving bat?

You will hit plastic 2-liter soda bottles with a wooden bat, a plastic bat, and a broom handle. A broom handle has less mass than a wooden bat, but you can swing it faster. Form a hypothesis as to whether a faster swinging bat or a slower, heavier bat will cause an empty plastic 2-liter soda bottle to travel farther when hit. With which bat will you be able to transfer more energy to the bottle?

Have extra bottles on hand in case any of them become too damaged to continue to be used in the experiment.

1 Place a small cardboard box or a shoe box on top of a stool. Set an empty plastic 2-liter soda bottle on the box. Be sure everyone is clear from the area before you swing. Using a wooden bat, hit the bottle with your hardest swing (see Figure 4). With a measuring tape, record the distance between the stool and where the bottle lands. Do this three times and take the average distance of the three hits. (To calculate the average distance, add the three distances together and divide the sum by 3.) This will help compensate for any differences in the swing each time.

2 Using a plastic bat, again hit a 2-liter bottle three times. Record each distance and calculate the average distance for the three hits.

3 Finally, use the wooden handle from an old broom to hit the bottle three times. The broom handle should be four feet or less in length. **Have an adult** help you use a hand saw to shorten the handle if necessary. Record each distance and find the average.

Compare the average distances of the three types of bats, and reach a conclusion about your hypothesis.

Softball is the most popular participant sport in the United States. About 40 million Americans will play at least one game of softball during a year.

FIGURE 4.
A heavy bat has more mass, but it takes more time to complete a swing. A lighter bat can be swung faster, but it has less mass. Which one will send the bottle farther?

SCIENCE PROJECT IDEAS

- Repeat the experiment using plastic 1-liter bottles. Do you expect there will be any significant difference in the distance you can hit the bottle?

- A bat has a "sweet spot," a place on the bat where, when a ball is hit there, the impact feels effortless to the batter and the maximum transfer of energy from the bat to the ball takes place. This spot is usually located six to eight inches from the end of a bat. Is there an optimum spot on a 2-liter plastic bottle (a "sweet spot") that would make it travel the farthest when hit (closer to the bottom, the middle, the top)?

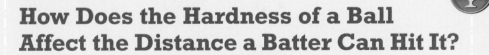

How Does the Hardness of a Ball Affect the Distance a Batter Can Hit It?

MATERIALS

- **an adult**
- baseball or softball
- batting tee
- baseball or softball bat
- measuring tape
- modeling clay
- a field

Baseballs and softballs are made up of layers of yarn over a rubber-coated cork center. They are designed to be fairly hard. Is this hardness important to how the ball receives a transfer of energy from a bat?

1 Place a ball on a batting tee (see Figure 5). Hit it as hard as you can with a bat. With a tape measure, measure the distance from the tee to where the ball stops.

2 Using modeling clay, form a round ball the same size as the baseball or softball. Place it on the batting tee and hit it as

Although the game of softball started in 1887, it wasn't until 1926 that it came to be called softball. Before then, it had been called "kitten ball," diamond ball," "mush ball," and "pumpkin ball."

FIGURE 5.
Place a ball on a batting tee. How far can you hit it? How far can you hit a ball made of clay?

hard as you can with the bat. Measure the distance the clay ball travels (or the biggest parts of it).

Compare the two distances. Did the harder ball travel farther than the softer clay ball? What happened to the energy from the bat that was transferred to the clay ball?

This project introduces another concept in physics called elasticity. An object is said to be highly elastic if it retains its shape, as do baseballs and softballs. A spring and a rubber band tend to be highly elastic objects. They jump back to their original shape when stretched and released. When a baseball or softball is hit by a bat, the ball may be slightly deformed for a fraction of a second, but it is quickly restored to its original shape. An object is said to be inelastic if it loses its original shape when a force is applied to it, as does clay.

SCIENCE PROJECT IDEAS

• Compare the distances you can hit balls of different densities and weights (a plastic ball, tennis ball, golf ball, rubber ball).

• Do a drop test on brand-new softballs or baseballs and compare their bounce to old, softened balls. How do the results compare?

EXPERIMENT **2.3**

Does the Distance Between Hands Placed on a Bat Affect the Distance of a Hit?

MATERIALS

- **an adult**
- baseball or softball bat
- 6 green tennis balls (or just mark "A" on 6 tennis balls with a marking pen)
- 6 orange tennis balls (or just mark "B" on 6 tennis balls with a marking pen)
- batting tee
- ruler

The position of a batter's hands on the bat handle is very important for accurate contact with the ball, and for maximum transfer of energy from the bat to the ball. Will you be able to hit a ball farther if your hands are split apart or close together?

1   Using a batting tee, hit 6 green tennis balls and 6 orange tennis balls, and alternate between green and orange. (This ensures that there will be more consistency batting each ball. You might get more tired by the time you hit the final few balls, and that would affect your swing.) Place your hands together, as shown in Figure 6a, when you hit the green balls, then split them with a 20-centimeter gap (about 8 inches) between them when hitting the orange balls (Figure 6b). Keep your batting stance constant, and try to use the same swing for all twelve balls.

2   To determine which grip position was best for hitting balls

FIGURE 6.
a. Batter with both hands together on a bat's handle.
b. Batter with hands 8 inches apart on bat handle.

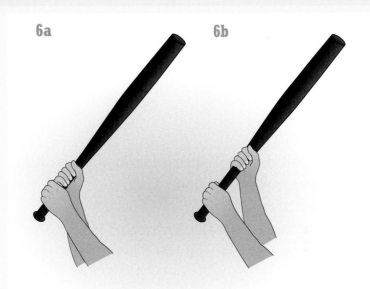

6a   6b

the farthest, you may not need to measure the distances. Simply look at where the green and orange balls lie in the field and draw a conclusion.

Based on your conclusion, how would you recommend a ballplayer grip the bat?

Keeping both hands together near the bottom of the bat (close to the knob at the handle's end) causes the opposite end to experience a "whip" effect, giving the bat maximum velocity.

SCIENCE PROJECT IDEA

Try varying the size of the gap between your hands and repeat the experiment.

EXPERIMENT **2.4**

How Does Striking a Ball Off-Center Differ From Hitting It Dead-Center?

MATERIALS

- **an adult**
- water
- several empty 1-liter plastic soda bottles
- field or open outdoor area
- stool
- shoe box or small cardboard box
- baseball or softball bat
- measuring tape

Ideally, a batter's goal is to hit the ball exactly at its center, where the ball's mass is the greatest. Remember, the ball has a rubber-coated cork center. This makes the center of the ball the most dense (density is mass, or amount of stuff, per volume). *Topping the ball* is a term used when the bat doesn't hit the ball squarely, but instead hits just the top piece of the ball (see Figure 7a).

Does hitting an object at a point where its density is less result in less transfer of energy?

1 Add water to a 1-liter plastic soda bottle until it is one quarter full. The water gives the bottle more mass at its bottom.

2 Outdoors, place the bottle on a small cardboard box or shoe box on top of a stool to raise it to a comfortable batting position (see Figure 7b).

3 Be sure everyone is clear from the area before you swing

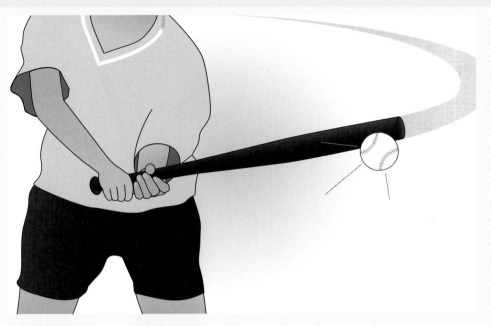

FIGURE 7A.
When a ball is hit off-center it is called topping the ball.

Tony Lazzeri of the New York Yankees certainly knew how to get the maximum transfer of energy from his bat to the ball. In 1936, he became the first player to achieve the amazing feat of hitting two grand slam home runs in a single game!

FIGURE 7B.
A plastic bottle partially filled with water has a density that is unevenly distributed.

the bat. With a bat, strike the bottle on its top half. Measure and record the distance the bottle travels from the stool.

You may notice that when you hit the bottle where it is less dense, some of the energy goes into making the bottle spin. This leaves less energy for making the bottle go far.

4 Perform this procedure three times, and calculate the

average distance the bottle travels. Have extra bottles handy in case one becomes too bashed.

5 Hit the bottle three more times, but this time hit it near its bottom. Measure and record the distances it travels.

Compare the average distances of the two trials. Were you able to hit the bottle farther when the bat struck the bottle where the mass was greater?

When a ball is hit off-center there is still some transfer of energy from the bat to the ball, but a lot of energy stays in the bat as it continues through the swing.

SCIENCE PROJECT IDEAS

• Repeat the experiment with the bottle half full of water. Compare your results to when the bottle was one-quarter full.

• A baseball, softball, tennis ball, and plastic Whiffle Ball all have different masses. When each is struck with a strong, identical force, will the balls that have more mass move farthest?

STATISTICS

Statistics are collections of facts about things or people. A lot of statistics are kept on ballplayers. In theory, by quantifying (expressing numerically) certain accomplishments of a ballplayer, it is easier to compare one player to another and to see how good, or how bad, a player is at a particular skill. These skills include hitting, fielding, pitching, and stealing bases. Batting average, for example, is a calculated number that can show the batting performance of a hitter. It is a fraction that stands for the number of times a batter gets a hit divided by the number of times the batter has been at bat. Another statistic, earned run average (ERA), shows how many runs, on average, a pitcher gives up per nine innings. Statistics are also kept for fielding, comparing the number of balls a player catches to those he or she mishandles that allow a runner to advance to another base.

43

The game of baseball has a long history of statistics. Henry Chadwick covered the game called cricket for local newspapers in the mid 1800s. By 1857, he had turned most of his attention to baseball, which has some similarities to cricket. He became known as the father of baseball because he developed many statistical formulas for the game. Chadwick strongly preached that statistics were the only way you could accurately understand the value of a player.

Statistics are important, and they have their useful place. But statistics do not always represent the true value of a ballplayer.

There are two main types of softball: fast-pitch and slow-pitch. In fast-pitch softball, the team is made up of nine players, and base stealing is allowed. The ball is pitched very fast, without an arc. At top speeds, a fast-pitch softball can travel over 100 km/hr! In slow-pitch softball, the team can have ten players, and base stealing is not allowed. The ball is pitched slower, and must have an arc. Slow-pitch softball is usually played on bigger fields than fast-pitch softball.

EXPERIMENT **3.1**

Can a Small Sample Accurately Represent the Larger Group?

MATERIALS

- bag or jar of assorted jelly beans, with at least 150 jelly beans
- pencil
- paper
- ruler
- a tray with a lip around the edge (to prevent things from rolling off)

One of the oldest and most common statistics is a player's batting average. The batting average is a ratio. It is calculated by dividing the number of hits by the number of times at bat (not including walks). If a batter walks, that turn at bat is not counted in "times at bat."

$$\frac{\text{number of hits}}{\text{times at bat}} = \text{batting average}$$

For example, if a player has come up to bat 20 times so far in a season and has gotten a hit 5 of those times, that player's batting average is .250, simply referred to as "two-fifty."

$$\frac{5}{20} = .250$$

A player with a batting average of .200 is getting one hit out of every five times at bat, because 1/5 = .200.

Batting average is used to compare the hitting ability of players. However, if a batter hasn't come up to bat very much, then the batting average is based on a very small sampling of information. When mathematicians and scientists want to get an accurate picture of the percentage of a particular object to a group of objects, they know that "sample size" is important. A large sample will give a more accurate estimate than a small sample.

If you flip a coin three times and it comes up heads two times out of three, it would appear that heads comes up more often than tails in coin tosses. But, that assumption is not true. There is a 50/50 chance that a tossed coin will come up heads or tails. The "sample size," which in this case is only three flips, is too small to give a true indication of what will happen if a coin is tossed many times. If you flip a coin 100 times, you will find that the number of times heads comes up is almost equal to the number of times tails comes up. If you based a statement on the results of tossing a coin only three times—and said that heads comes up two thirds of the time—then your statement would be wrong.

At the beginning of a baseball season, after only a few games have been played, each player will have been up to bat less than ten times. Trying to calculate the batting average for such a player would give an inaccurate indication of how good or bad a hitter he is. A player coming up to bat only once and striking out has a batting average of zero. If he had gotten a hit, then his average would be 1.000. You may have heard the phrase *batting a thousand*. Looking at the batting average for only this first time at bat would give an incorrect conclusion as to the batting ability of this player.

Hypothesize that you cannot determine an accurate percentage of an object in a group of objects unless the sample size is sufficiently large. Therefore, batting average cannot be an accurate estimate of a player's batting ability unless he has been up to bat many times.

1 Open a bag of jelly beans that contains different colored beans. Make sure the bag contains an even mix of different colors. (For example, if the bag is mostly red, with just a few beans of other colors, it will not be appropriate for

Color	# of beans (10 sampled)	"Batting average" (10 sampled)	# of beans (100 sampled)	"Batting average" (100 sampled)
Blue				
Green				
Purple				
Red				
Yellow				

DO NOT WRITE IN THIS BOOK

FIGURE 8.
Draw a chart (or use a spreadsheet program on a computer) to record and compare your results of sampling jelly beans.

this experiment.) Using a ruler and a piece of paper, make a chart, as shown in Figure 8, that has five columns and six rows—one for each color. If your bag has less than six colors, your chart will have fewer rows, and if it has more than six colors, add another row for each color.

2 Without looking, reach into the bag and pull out 10 beans. Under the column heading "# of beans (10 sampled)," write the number of beans in each row by its color.

Let's assume each color is a baseball or softball player (Mr. Blue, Ms. Green, etc.). The sample size represents the number of times each player has come up to bat, and the colored beans represent hits.

Calculate the "batting average" for each player by dividing the number of beans for each color by 10, and place the result in the column marked "Batting average (10 sampled)." For example, if there are two blue beans, then 2 divided by 10 equals .2, or .200 (batting average is usually expressed with three places beyond the decimal point).

3 Next, put those 10 beans back into the bag, close the bag, and shake. Now, randomly pick out 100 beans and place them on a tray that has a lip to keep them from rolling off. Count the number of each color and fill in the column on your chart labeled "# of beans (100 sampled)." Again, calculate the "batting average" based on 100 times "at bat."

Compare the "batting average" of each color from the small sample size of 10 to that of the sample of 100. Is there a big difference between the numbers?

4 Prove that a sample size of 100 gives a more accurate result by dumping the beans back into the bag, shaking it, and counting out another 100 beans. Are the results of the averages from the two large-sample trials closer to each other than to the average based on a sample size of only 10?

Based on your experiment, you can understand why you cannot accurately predict which ballplayers will have a good batting season with batting averages calculated from the player's performance in only the first few games of the season.

SCIENCE PROJECT IDEAS

- Use a computer spreadsheet program to set up your chart and automatically calculate batting averages. Create a graph showing the results.

- Is a large sample also important for determining other baseball statistics such as fielding errors?

- Follow the batting average of your favorite ballplayers in a daily newspaper during baseball season. Does their average change much throughout the season?

EXPERIMENT 3.2

Batting Average and the True Value of a Hitter

The batting average statistic may not be the best measure of a ballplayer's performance as a hitter. As was explained in Experiment 3.1, batting average is calculated by dividing the number of hits by the number of times at bat. Two ballplayers may have the same batting average, and yet one may be a much more valuable player when it comes to batting performance.

A player with a batting average of .200 is getting one hit out of every five times at bat, because 1/5 = .200. But that average assumes that every hit is the same. What if one of those two players gets a single every time he or she gets a hit, but the other player gets a home run every time he or she gets a hit? If you base the value of those players only on their batting average statistics, you would think they are both about equal. But, which player would you rather have on your team, the one who hits singles, or the one who hits home runs?

There is another batting average statistic, called slugging percentage. It takes into account the type of hit a batter gets. Each time a player gets a hit, there is a number assigned to it: 1 if the batter gets a single, 2 for a double, 3 for a triple, and 4 for a home run. In the standard batting average equation, where the number of hits is divided by the number of times at bat, number of hits will be replaced by your new "weighted" number. Instead of simply assigning a value of 1 every time a player gets a hit, assign a number from 1 to 4. This new weighted batting average will be larger than traditional batting averages. For example, suppose a player comes up to bat five times. The first two times he strikes out (assign a zero for each). The third time he gets a single (assign a 1); the fourth time he hits a triple (assign a 3) and the fifth time he hits a double (assign a 2). His slugging percentage is:

$$\frac{0 + 0 + 1 + 3 + 2}{5 \text{ (the number of times at bat)}} = \frac{6}{5}, \text{ or } 1.200.$$

1 To apply your new slugging percentage statistic, attend several baseball or softball games, local Little League games, or ball games at your school (the more games from which you gather data the better, preferably the whole season). Instead of attending local ball games, you may be able to get the necessary statistics you need for your favorite ball team from sports newspapers, magazines, or the Internet. Keep a record of each player, the number of times at bat, and assign a weighted hit number for each hit.

2 After gathering a sufficient amount of data, compare the

The all-time leader in career batting average is Ty Cobb, with .366. Babe Ruth comes in tenth with .342. Tip O'Neill of the St. Louis Browns comes in first place of those with the highest batting average in a single season, when in 1887 he batted .485.

slugging percentage statistics to those calculated using the standard batting average formula.

3 Set up a computer spreadsheet program to enter, calculate, and report each player's slugging percentage, and compare it to the standard batting average. Which one is more effective in describing a player's hitting ability?

SCIENCE PROJECT IDEAS

- The batting average statistic also has other flaws in accurately assessing a player's batting ability. For example, it doesn't take into account walks and times when a batter makes a sacrifice out (fly balls or bunts) in order to advance a base runner. Can you think of additional ways the value of the batting average statistic could be improved? How about accounting for times when a batter gets on base because of a fielding error?

- Earned run average and fielding percentage are some other statistics used in baseball and softball. Learn about how these averages are calculated, and think of ways these statistics could be improved.

- What other sports use statistics? How are they the same and different from the baseball and softball statistics? What statistics pertain to the entire team rather than just to individual players?

FRICTION AND PRESSURE

Friction is the resistance that objects have to being moved across another surface. Sometimes we try to reduce friction, and sometimes we try to increase friction. When moving parts of a machine come in contact with each other, oil or some other lubricant is used to reduce friction, which makes them work more efficiently. When a car needs to drive on slippery, icy roads, chains may be placed on the tires to increase friction with the road and keep the car from sliding. Chalk is used on the end of cue sticks in the games of pool and billiards to increase friction between the cue stick and billiard ball. Ping-Pong paddles are coated with rubber to increase friction between the paddles and the ball.

A pitcher wants friction between his hand and the ball. A sweaty hand could cause a pitcher to lose control of the ball when throwing it. Pitchers may use a rosin bag to increase friction in their pitching hands. Rosin makes their hands sticky.

Batters want friction between their hands and the bat. They don't want the bat to slip out of their hands, but want to keep a firm grip. Batters may use batting gloves that increase friction to give them a better grip on the bat.

Base runners want friction between their feet and the ground, so when they push off the ground or run, they won't slip. Ballplayers wear shoes with cleats to make better contact with the ground.

Can you think of other sports where increasing or decreasing friction is helpful to playing the game?

EXPERIMENT **4.1**

How Do Shoes Affect a Runner's Speed?

Traction is the amount of friction between an object and the surface upon which it is moving. When running, it is desirable to have as much traction as possible. Have you ever tried to run fast on beach sand? You know it is harder than running on a concrete sidewalk. There is more friction between your shoes and solid concrete than between your shoes and shifting sand.

To increase traction when running on dirt or grass, many people playing sports such as soccer, track, and baseball or softball wear shoes with cleats (see Figure 9). Cleats are studs on the bottom of shoes to assist in gripping the ground. Shoes with cleats help prevent slipping when running, and help give quicker starts. Cleats have better traction because the force of the runner's body weight is concentrated into the small, pointed surfaces of the many cleats on the shoes, instead of being spread out over the flat bottom of a shoe. Once all those points are firmly in the ground, there is more surface area in contact with the ground. Since the key to friction is how much surface area is in contact with another surface, cleats give a better grip.

FIGURE 9.
Both baseball and softball players wear shoes with cleats to improve their running performance. Cleats are made of metal and plastic. For safety reasons, metal cleats are not allowed in Little League.

Will wearing shoes with cleats help you and your teammates run faster?

1 Find a clear, open area where you can run 90 feet straight, without having to turn. In baseball, the distance between home plate and first base is 90 feet, so you can use home plate as the starting point and first base as the ending point. If you don't have access to a field, just mark a distance of about 90 feet with a starting and finishing line.

2 Have several friends run the distance wearing flat shoes or sneakers, and then have them run the same path again wearing properly fitting shoes with cleats. Record the time of each run using a stopwatch. Compare the times. Were the times shorter when your friends were wearing cleats compared to when they were wearing flat-bottom shoes?

3 For a visual comparison, draw a vertical bar chart to represent the time of each run.

SCIENCE PROJECT IDEAS

• Use a computer spreadsheet program to record the times and compare them. Have the spreadsheet program print a graph comparing times. Do the results change for longer or shorter distances?

• In order to run the shortest distance around the bases, a runner must turn quickly, and not overrun the base. Do shoes with cleats help in changing direction quickly?

EXPERIMENT **4.2**

Does a Spinning Ball Travel in a Straight or Curved Path?

MATERIALS
- **an adult**
- drill with a bit whose diameter is smaller than the diameter of the shaft on the screw eye
- baseball or softball
- eye screw
- about 6 meters (20 feet) of string
- scissors
- the swivel connector from a fishing leader line
- 4- or 5-foot 2-by-4 board
- a friend

Pitching is one of the most important aspects of baseball and softball. Professional pitchers learn how to throw in different ways to affect how the ball behaves. The ball is not perfectly round because it has stitches, which are raised surfaces. The stitches can disrupt the flow of air around the ball, causing it to move in different ways. Do you think a spinning baseball or softball will travel in a different path compared to one that is not spinning? Make a hypothesis.

To test your hypothesis, you will swing a baseball or softball on a string like a pendulum. For one trial the ball will be spinning, and for the next it will not.

1 Have an adult use a drill to make a small starter hole in a ball. Then screw an eye screw into the ball.

2 Tie a 14-centimeter (6-inch) piece of string to the swivel connector of a fishing leader line (see Figure 10a).

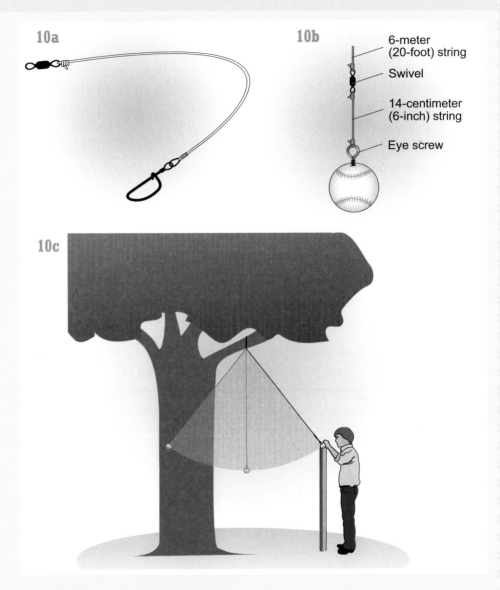

10a

10b
- 6-meter (20-foot) string
- Swivel
- 14-centimeter (6-inch) string
- Eye screw

10c

FIGURE 10.

a. The swivel connector of a fishing leader line.

b. Screw an eye screw into a ball and tie it to a leader line swivel.

c. Use a 2-by-4 as a reference to ensure the ball is released from the same height each time. Look for lateral movement in the ball's swinging path.

A leader line can be purchased inexpensively from a bait-and-tackle shop, or you may be able to borrow one from a fisherman friend.

3 Tie the other end of the short piece of string to the screw eye in the ball. On the other end of the leader line swivel, tie a 6-meter (20-foot) piece of string (see Figure 10b). The leader line swivel turns freely, so you will be able to spin the ball without having the long piece of string twist with it.

4 Holding one end of the string, throw the ball with the string attached to it over a high branch on a tree. The branch should be about 3 meters (9 or 10 feet) off the ground. Tie the other end of the string to a lower branch or anything else that will hold it securely. Now the ball can swing like a pendulum from the branch.

5 To start the ball pendulum swinging, pull back on the string. You will need to release the ball from the same height each time you let it begin swinging. To do this, you could use a 4- or 5-foot piece of 2-by-4 lumber (a stud) and pull the string back until the ball is the same height as the stud standing in an upright position (see Figure 10c).

Major league pitchers learn to throw knuckle-balls, sliders, curveballs, screwballs, and other types, but most coaches recommend that Little League ballplayers stick to straight pitches. Throwing fancy types of balls may cause injuries to elbows and wrists.

6 Make sure the ball is not moving. Then let go of the string to begin the ball swinging. Stand so that you can see the ball coming toward you and swinging away from you. That will enable you to observe any lateral (side-to-side) motion. Does the ball travel back and forth in a straight path or is there lateral motion?

7 Pull the string back again and position it at the same starting height. While you are holding the string just above the swivel connector, have a friend place the ball between his or her hands and impart a spin on the ball. Do this by placing the palms of the hands on each side of the ball. Swiftly move one hand forward and one backward. Steady the ball so that it is spinning on its axis, but not swinging side to side. Then let go of the string and observe the back-and-forth path it travels.

Does the ball travel back and forth in a straight path, or is there any lateral motion?

The reason a pitcher can throw a ball that curves is a result of Bernoulli's principle. Daniel Bernoulli, a Swiss mathematician, discovered over two hundred years ago that air pressure changes with speed. Engineers apply the principle when building airplanes. As an airplane moves forward, air flows over the top of and under the wings. The shape of the wings makes the air that flows over the top travel farther than the air flowing underneath. The air on top of the wings, then, travels faster, which creates a lower air pressure. This creates lift for the plane, and it moves off the ground, toward the area of less pressure.

In a similar way, the stitches on a ball interact with the air as the ball moves through it. The stitches on a spinning ball cause the air pressure to be different on one side than the other. When pressure is lower on one side, the ball will drift in the direction of less pressure. This will cause a curve, or lateral motion.

You may want to learn more about aerodynamics, which is a branch of physics that studies air as it moves against objects and objects as they move through air.

SCIENCE PROJECT IDEA

Does it make a difference in the path of the baseball or softball if the ball is spinning clockwise or counterclockwise?

EXPERIMENT 4.3

Can a Batting Glove Help Your Hitting?

> **MATERIALS**
> - batting glove
> - a friend
> - an inside door that has a doorknob on both sides, such as a bedroom door

Batters want to increase the friction between their hands and the bat to keep the bat from slipping. Some ballplayers claim batting gloves increase friction, helping them hit better by giving them a better grip on the bat handle. Can you show how a batting glove increases friction with the object it comes in contact with?

1 To see how a batting glove increases friction, have a friend stand on one side of an inside door of your house, such as a bedroom door. Ask her to hold the doorknob with one hand. Stand on the other side and hold the doorknob with one hand. Leave the door open so that you can see each other.

2 Have your friend turn the doorknob, while you try to keep your knob from turning.

  Were you able to keep the knob from turning, or to at least make it hard for your friend to turn?

3 Now put a batting glove on your hand (see Figure 11). Again, have your friend turn the doorknob while you try to keep it from turning. Were you able to keep the knob from turning, or at least make it harder than before for your friend to turn the knob? Why do you think this happened?

It used to be legal to apply pine tar to a bat's handle to increase friction. On July 19, 1975, New York Yankee catcher Thurman Munson hit a single that allowed a runner to score, but the umpire ruled Munson was out. He said the pine tar extended too far up the handle; it should not exceed 18 inches from the end. The umpire took the run off the score in what turned out to be a one-run loss (the opposing team was the Minnesota Twins).

FIGURE 11.
Hold a doorknob while wearing a batting glove, and have a friend try to turn the knob from the other side. Does the batting glove give you a better grip?

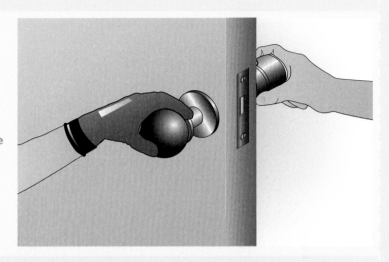

In physics, the term *torque* is used to describe a force in a rotating or turning direction. When you twist the handle of a screwdriver, you are applying a rotational force. When your friend tried to turn the doorknob, he or she was applying torque.

Sometimes widemouthed pickle jars can be hard to open. Would a batting glove help increase friction to get a better grip on the jar's lid?

SCIENCE PROJECT IDEA

Instead of increasing friction on your side by wearing a batting glove, reduce the friction on your friend's side. Apply three or four drops of baby oil to a paper towel and wipe the doorknob on your friend's side. Have your friend try to turn the doorknob again while you hold the other knob.

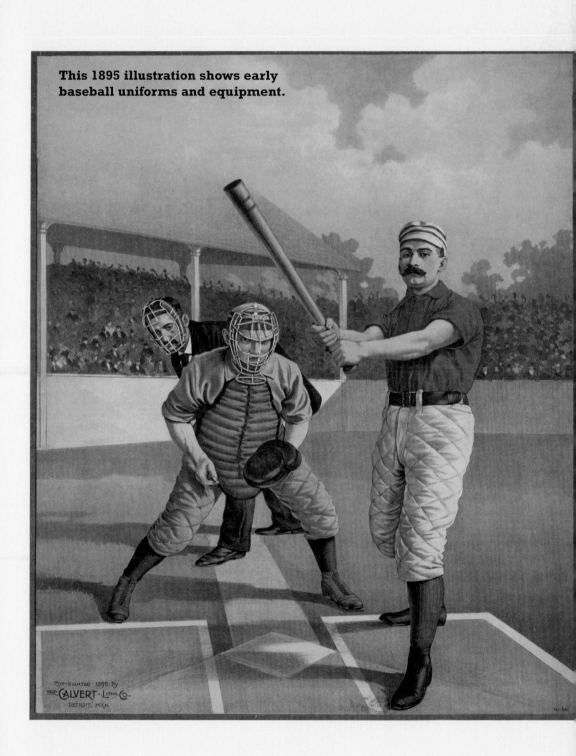

This 1895 illustration shows early baseball uniforms and equipment.

COPYRIGHTED 1895 BY
THE CALVERT · LITHO · CO.
DETROIT, MICH.

BAT USE

Baseball is a very old game. It has been played since the 1800s. When the game first became popular, people were still getting around on horses and in carriages. In fact, when cars were invented and people no longer used horses and buggies, wagon tongues were made into baseball bats. (Wagon tongues are long, heavy boards on the front of wagons, where the horses were hitched.) These early bats were heavy and flat. As years went by, baseball bats became more tapered.

By the 1950s, pitchers were becoming very skilled. They were able to throw fastballs with more speed. To hit a fastball, the batter had to be able to swing a bat fast, so lighter-weight bats became popular.

A bat must feel just right to a batter to do his best when hitting. The famous baseball player Lou Brock of the St. Louis Cardinals once said, "Your bat is your life." "Shoeless

Joe" Jackson of the Chicago White Sox actually slept with his bat. Ballplayers all have their favorites. Babe Ruth's favorite bats had knots in them.

Work with your coach to help find the best bat for you. It will improve your performance and your enjoyment of the game.

The first game of softball was played inside a gym in 1887, where Harvard and Yale fans had gathered during a football game. A Yale supporter playfully picked up a boxing glove and threw it at a Harvard fan, who hit it with a stick. This gave George Hancock the idea for the game of softball.

EXPERIMENT 5.1

Which Bat Weight Is Best for You?

MATERIALS
- batting helmet
- a partner
- baseball or softball
- use of a ball field or open field
- one lightweight bat
- one medium-weight bat
- one heavy bat
- paper and pencil

Baseball and softball bats are made in different weights (from about 15 to 30 ounces). Does matching the proper-weight bat to the players help them be better hitters?

1 Put on a batting helmet. Have a partner throw pitches to you while you use bats of different weights. The pitcher should be someone who can throw the ball through the strike zone consistently, and not with any speed or curves. Have the pitcher throw 10 strikes while you use a light-weight bat, 10 while you use a medium-weight bat, and 10 while you use a heavy-weight bat.

2 Write down the number of times you hit the ball with each bat. Were you able to hit the ball more times with one bat than another?

To practice swinging before stepping into the batter's box, ballplayers as far back as the early 1900s would swing two bats. Then when they stepped up to home plate, their bat would feel lighter and easier to swing. In the 1960s the donut became commonly used in place of the second bat. The donut is a weight that slips on the end of the bat to make it heavier. Now, weighted bats are used, with the weight evenly distributed along these "warm-up bats."

EXPERIMENT 5.2

Does Swinging Early or Late Determine the Direction of a Hit?

MATERIALS

- **an adult**
- drill with ¾-inch bit
- ½-inch-diameter wooden dowel, 8 inches long
- 1-square-foot piece of plywood, ¾ inch thick
- several thick washers
- 2 nails
- hammer
- empty paper towel roll
- several books
- rubber band
- Ping-Pong ball

In golf and T-ball, the ball sits still until it is hit. In baseball and softball, a pitcher throws the ball to the batter. It is more difficult to hit a moving ball. It is even more difficult to determine which direction the ball will go once it is hit. Does the direction a hit ball travels depend on whether the bat is swung early or late?

A batter has less than one second to decide if the pitched ball is a good pitch, and then to start swinging the bat. Timing the swing is critical. If a batter swings too early or too late, he'll be swinging at empty air. If a ball is hit by an early swing, to which field is it more likely to go: right field, center field, or left field? If a ball is hit by a late swing, to which field is it more likely to go? (Of course, its direction also depends on whether the batter is left- or right-handed.)

You can build a device to simulate a bat swinging early and

late. A Ping-Pong ball will be rolled toward a wooden dowel that is connected to a rubber band. The wooden dowel can be pulled back and released early (before the ball reaches it) or late (when the ball is just about past it).

1   Construct the device shown in Figure 12. **Have an adult drill a hole near one end of a ½-inch wooden dowel.** The hole in the dowel should be bigger than a nail so that the dowel can freely pivot on the nail.

2   On a piece of 1-foot-square plywood, stack several thick washers on top of each other. Place the drilled hole of the wooden dowel on top of the washers. **Place a nail through the holes in the dowel and in the washers, then hammer the nail a little way into the wood.** The washers will lift the dowel off the plywood so that it can swing with less friction, and so that it will hit the Ping-Pong ball squarely in its center.

3   Make a ramp from an empty paper towel roll sitting between two stacks of books. Move the stacks slightly apart so that the paper towel roll can sit down in the gap to be held steady.

4   **Hammer another nail partly into the plywood** several inches from the nail in the wooden dowel. Place a rubber band around the second nail and the wooden dowel.

5   Pull back on the wooden dowel so that the rubber band is stretched. Place a Ping-Pong ball in the paper towel roll and let it roll down toward the dowel. Do this 10 times, each time letting go of the dowel well before the ball gets to it (simulating a batter swinging early).

6   Do it another 10 times, each time letting go of the dowel when the ball is very close to the dowel (simulating a batter swinging late).

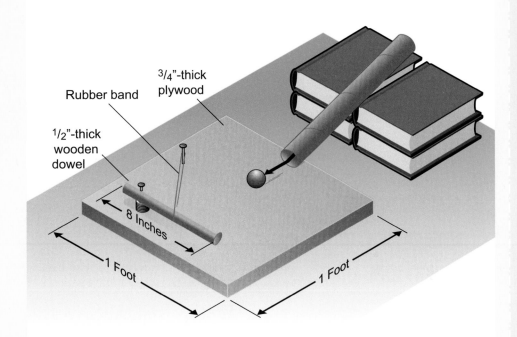

Rubber band

3/4"-thick plywood

1/2"-thick wooden dowel

8 Inches

1 Foot

1 Foot

FIGURE 12.
You can construct a device that will simulate a bat hitting a ball with an early swing and a late swing.

Is there one direction that the ball seems to go most of the time when the dowel is swung early? Is there one direction that the ball seems to go most of the time when the dowel is swung late? How does this relate to a batter and his swing? This setup simulates a right-handed batter. What if the batter is left-handed? To which field will the ball travel if a left-handed batter swings early? Late?

SCIENCE PROJECT IDEA

Using a protractor and drawing tools, show the direction a ball is more likely to take when a ball is hit too early and when it is hit too late. In physics, lines that show a direction and a magnitude (such as speed) are called vectors.

EXPERIMENT 5.3

Does "Choking Up" on the Bat Increase Bat Control?

MATERIALS

- use of a clear field area
- 5 friends
- bat
- baseball or softball
- batting tee
- pencil and paper

In baseball and softball, "choking up" on the bat is when the batter grasps the bat farther up on the bat's gripping end. Most ballplayers hold both hands together down by the knob end of the bat (Figure 13a). Holding the bat in this position enables the batter to swing with the most force. However, choking up on the bat increases a batter's control of his or her swing—but the bat cannot be swung with quite as much power (Figure 13b).

Does choking up on the bat give your teammates better control of the bat, increasing their batting averages?

Don't tell your friends ahead of time what you are doing, so they won't be predispositioned (inclined to make the results come out a certain way). Be sure the area is clear before each batter swings.

1 Gather five friends or teammates. Have each friend hold a bat with their hands together, down by the knob. Have them try to hit the ball from a batting tee 10 times. Record the number of times they hit the ball.

2 Now, have each friend choke up on the bat, and ask them

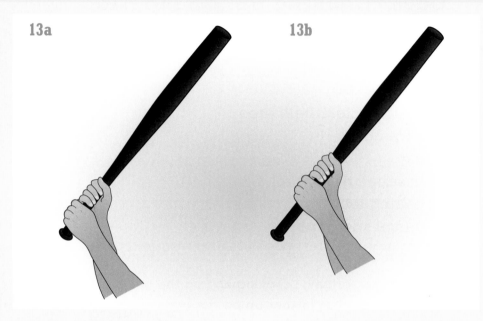

FIGURE 13.

a. A bat is normally held with two hands near the knob at the tapered end of the bat.

b. Choking up on the bat is when both hands are moved up the gripping end, away from the knob.

to try to hit the ball 10 times. Record the number of times they hit the ball.

3 Compare the number of times each friend hit the ball while holding the bat in the two different positions. Did they get more hits when they choked up?

4 Try the experiment again, but this time record the accuracy of their swings. It's important that they not only hit the ball, but also that they hit the ball well. Just hitting the ball in a game isn't good enough. A player should not hit the batting tee or top the ball. How many times do your friends hit it squarely and make good contact?

SCIENCE PROJECT IDEA

One of the simple machines in physics is the lever. A lever is a straight arm or bar that is used to do work. There are three types of levers: first class, second class, and third class. Each has a fulcrum (or pivot point), a point where a force is applied, and placement of a load (something that is to be moved). A seesaw in playgrounds is a type of lever. Depending on where the fulcrum and load are placed and the point at which a force is applied, each lever has a different effect on how the load is moved. Explain how swinging a bat, where your hands act as a fulcrum, is an example of a type of lever.

Baseballs are sewn by hand, and each ball has 108 stitches, with the first and last stitches being cleverly hidden. Yet, for all the work that goes into manufacturing it, the average life of a major league baseball is only six pitches!

CREATIVE BASEBALL AND SOFTBALL

As with any sport, there is a lot that goes on behind the scenes by athletes preparing for a game. To be a good ballplayer, an athlete needs to do more than show up at the field on the day of a game. A serious athlete will spend a lot of time practicing to improve his or her skills. A ballplayer may develop creative ways of practicing the different skills needed for the game. In this chapter, we will explore some creative ideas for practice.

Practice is more than just working out with the team. A ballplayer can also work out individually. Many athletes cross train, which means they participate in sports other than their main sport as a way to help them play their chosen sport better. For example, playing tennis and Ping-Pong may improve hand-eye coordination, which could help with batting. Running track can improve baserunning and the ability to quickly change direction when running from one base to another. Weight lifting will strengthen arms and legs, thus increasing the ability to run, throw, and swing a bat.

Practice, both with the team and individually, is important to improving your baseball and softball skills. You will enjoy the game more if you can become a better player. But most of all, remember that the game needs to be fun! Practicing hard and working out is good, but be sure to make those times enjoyable, too.

And always remember good sportsmanship. It is a great feeling of accomplishment to win a ball game. But even when you lose, you should have had lots of fun just playing the game!

EXPERIMENT 6.1

Where Within the Strike Zone Is Your Strongest Swing?

MATERIALS
- cardboard box a little more than ½ meter high (about 2 feet)
- 4 or 5 bricks
- empty paper towel roll
- modeling clay
- baseball or softball
- bat

The strike zone covers an area from just below the batter's knees to his armpits. When a batter swings within the strike zone but with no ball being pitched, does the batter tend to swing through the same spot most of the time? Every individual may have a height at which that player's bat tends to stay when swung. If batters can determine the height of their natural swing, this would be useful to them. They would look for pitches at that height to increase their odds of getting a good hit.

1 Construct a homemade batting tee that has a variable height. The base will be a cardboard box about ½ meter (2 feet) high. Stack several bricks on top of the box. The bricks should be lying down with their broadsides parallel to the ground (they are the most stable in this position).

2 Place an empty paper towel roll on the top brick, and mold some modeling clay around it to help it stand up. Set a baseball or softball on top of the paper towel roll (see Figure 14). This homemade batting tee can be raised or lowered by simply adding or taking away bricks.

Clay
Brick
Box

FIGURE 14.
A homemade batting tee with variable height will help you find the height of your natural swing.

3 Be sure everyone is clear of the area before you swing the bat. Step up to the tee. Looking straight ahead as if you were looking at a pitcher about to throw a ball, swing your bat. Don't look at the ball on the homemade batting tee.

4 If your swing goes over the top of the ball, add another brick to the stack to raise it. If your swing hits the paper towel roll, remove one of the bricks to lower the ball. Set the ball on top of the roll and swing again.

5 Continue adding or removing bricks until you are hitting the ball most of the time. Observe where this height is in relation to your body. Could this be the height of a pitch that's best for you?

6 You could zone in on an even more accurate height by using paper towel rolls cut at different heights.

SCIENCE PROJECT IDEA

A musician sometimes practices by playing a song in his head, envisioning where his fingers will be placed on his instrument. Can you improve your game while thinking about it before you go to sleep?

In the very early days of baseball, strikes were counted only if the batter swung and missed. Balls weren't counted at all, so sometimes it would take hours just to play three innings. There were many changes in the rules, but by 1889 it was settled that the umpire would call every pitch as either a ball or a strike, and three strikes and four balls was the limit. Before 1889, there hadn't been a need to determine a strike zone. Since then, the width of the strike zone has always been the width of home plate, but the height has changed. In 1969 it was defined as the distance between the armpits and the top of the knees. It was changed again in 1996 to extend to the bottom of the knees.

EXPERIMENT 6.2

What Is the Fastest Way to Get the Ball From Deep Center Field to Home Plate?

MATERIALS
- 2 baseballs or softballs
- 3 friends
- baseball glove
- batting helmet
- use of a ball field

When a ball is hit deep into the outfield and the team at bat has runners on base, the outfielder must quickly get the ball back to the infield. This is especially important when there is a runner on third base heading for home.

It's a very long distance from deep in the outfield to home plate. A ball could not be thrown that distance in a straight line, because gravity would pull the ball to the ground long before it had time to reach home plate. Even if an outfielder were capable of throwing a ball that distance, he or she would have to throw it in a high arc to avoid it rolling on the ground.

However, by throwing a ball in a high arc, the ball must cover more distance than it would if it traveled in a straighter line. Extra time is needed for the ball to cover the extra distance.

It wasn't until the mid-1890s that the strategy of using a cutoff man to relay the ball became widespread. A cutoff player would be either the second baseman, shortstop, or even the pitcher—whoever could get in a position to receive a throw from an outfielder, turn, and quickly throw the ball to the catcher at home plate. This cutoff play was one of the revolutionary strategies that eventually became common practice.

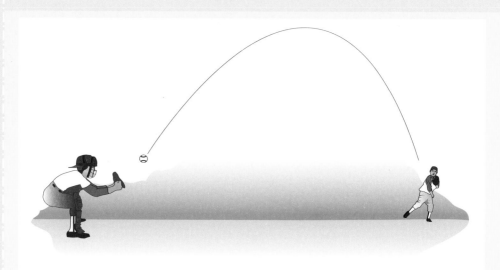

FIGURE 15.
In order to throw a ball a long distance without letting it roll on the ground, the ball must be thrown in a high arc. This increases the distance the ball must travel, so it takes more time than if the ball could be thrown in a straighter path.

This experiment will determine if it is faster to get a ball from the outfield to home plate with one throw or by using the relay method.

1 Position two people deep in center field, each holding a ball.

2 Position another person by second base, wearing a baseball glove. This relay person should have the ability to catch and throw well.

3 Stand near home plate, but off to one side. Wear a batting helmet for safety.

4 Shout, "Ready, set, throw!" to signal both outfielders to throw their balls. One outfielder should aim for home plate, throwing the ball in a high arc (Figure 15). The other outfielder should aim for the relay person, throwing the ball with as little arc as possible.

5 Let the outfielder's ball bounce and roll all the way to home plate if it is no longer airborne. The cutoff player by second base must make a clean catch, turn quickly, and make an accurate throw toward home plate.

6 From your position near home plate, observe which ball arrives at home plate first.

7 Repeat at least three times. What do your results show?

It wasn't until the end of the 1860s that outfield fences became common in professional ballparks. In the very early days, the game was played on open fields, and the outfielders had some long runs to get a ball that was hit past them. They also had some long throws to get the ball back to the infield. Today, when an infielder sees the ball go over his or her head, that player will immediately get into a position to relay the ball from the outfielder to home plate.

PRACTICE IDEA

The lower the arc when throwing a ball, the better, but you don't want the ball to bounce off the ground on its way to the cutoff player. Contact with the ground will slow the ball and also make it hard to catch. Here's a great practice exercise and friendly competition. Have three players stand together (as though they were in an outfield), and place a baseball or softball on the ground in front of each player. Position three players next to each other within a comfortable throwing distance from them (simulating cutoff players). Place three more players together (representing where a catcher would be at home plate), and again position them within throwing distance of the cutoff players. This sets up three "teams" of an outfielder, his cutoff player, and his catcher at home plate. Have someone yell, "Ready, set, go!" Then, each outfielder must pick up the ball, throw it to his corresponding cutoff player, who will then catch the ball, turn as quickly as possible, and make an accurate throw to his catcher at home plate. Make it a competition by seeing which team can get the ball to the catcher the fastest. The winning team is the best out of seven times. This would also make a good tryout exercise for assigning positions on a team.

EXPERIMENT **6.3**

Can You Improve Your Pitching to the Extreme Edges of the Strike Zone?

MATERIALS
- **an adult**
- backyard or park
- shovel or posthole digger
- tape measure
- two 2-by-4 studs, 5 or 6 feet long
- a friend
- marking pen
- scissors
- paper plate
- 8 pushpins or thumbtacks
- baseball or softball
- catcher's gear (optional)

The challenge of a pitcher is to throw the ball through the strike zone, but not where the batter wants it. You can build a simple practice device for pitching balls through the four corners of the strike zone.

The strike zone is defined as the area over home plate and just below a batter's knees up to the armpits. Different players are different heights, so there will be some slight change in the strike zone height, depending on the player. The width of the strike zone is always the same, 17 inches, which is the width of home plate.

1 Get permission to dig two holes that you will fill back in after your experiment. (The experiment can be done in your backyard or neighborhood park.) Using a shovel or

posthole digger, dig two small holes 17 inches apart and about one foot deep. They only need to be a few inches wide so that a 2-by-4 stud can be placed in them vertically.

2 Place a 5- or 6-foot 2-by-4 stud in each hole and fill in dirt around them. The gap between them must be 17 inches and they must be at least tall enough to come up to your armpits once they are in the ground.

3 In Little League, the pitcher's mound is 46 feet from home plate. Measure this distance from the studs and mark a spot on the ground where the pitcher will stand.

4 Have a friend stand next to the studs. Take a marking pen and mark a spot on each stud that is just below your

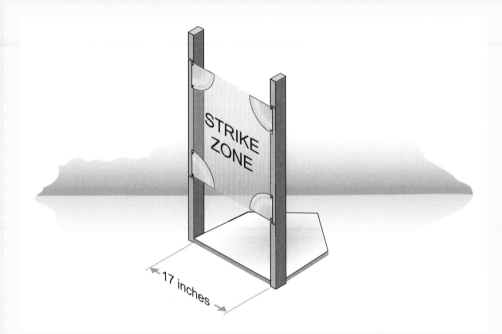

FIGURE 16.
The pitcher must learn to throw the ball in the strike zone, but not where the batter wants it.

There are over thirty teams in the National Wheelchair Softball Association—many of which are sponsored by Major League Baseball teams, such as the Boston Red Sox, Philadelphia Phillies, Chicago Cubs, and New York Mets.

friend's knees and a spot on each at the height of his or her armpits.

5 With a pair of scissors, cut a paper plate into quarters. Using pushpins or thumbtacks, mount each quarter of the paper plate at the two top and two bottom markings, as shown in Figure 16. These pieces should be inside the strike zone, but at the inside corner boundaries.

6 Practice pitching the ball, aiming to hit the plates. You may want to have a backboard behind your practice device to stop the ball, or have a friend with a catcher's mitt and proper protective gear practice their catching skills behind your device. Be careful! A pitched ball that hits one of the 2-by-4 studs may fly in any direction.

EXPERIMENT **6.4**

Can You Make Up Your Own Game That Will Improve Your Baseball or Softball Skills?

MATERIALS

- baseball field
- cardboard box about 1 meter (3 feet) high
- an empty plastic 3-liter soda bottle
- a friend
- batting helmet
- several baseballs or softballs
- bat

Baseball and softball are team sports, but they also depend on the skills of each individual. It is hard to get a whole team of friends together to practice all the time. During those times when there is only you and a friend, make up games that the two of you can play that would also help your baseball or softball skills.

1   Take a cardboard box that is about 1 meter (3 feet) high and set it about 1 meter behind home plate. On top of the box, place an empty plastic 3-liter soda bottle.

2   Have your friend stand on the pitcher's mound. You will stand in the batter's box, wearing a batting helmet. Your friend will pitch the ball and try to knock down the soda bottle. You will try to hit the ball (Figure 17).

3   If you hit the ball anywhere in fair territory, consider it to be a single. No one will be running any bases. If your friend knocks the bottle over, it is an out. Don't count the times

FIGURE 17.

You can invent your own version of baseball or softball where you need only two players. Make up your own set of rules. Such games can also help you build skills needed for playing baseball or softball.

when the bottle falls over because the box is hit. You may want to have a bunch of balls, so you won't need to keep chasing the hits and throwing the ball back to the pitcher.

4 After three outs, switch places so that you are now pitching and your friend is batting. You can play a 9-inning game. This game requires only two people, and each will get a chance to practice both pitching and batting.

After playing this new game for a while, do your baseball or softball skills improve? How could you keep track of some of your individual statistics to see whether this game improved your hitting or fielding?

SCIENCE PROJECT IDEAS

- Make up a complete set of rules for your game, such as what happens when a ball is hit foul.

- Create a game that counts only the hits that go in a certain direction, such as toward third base or into right field.

This made-up game is somewhat similar to the game of cricket, where a pitcher tries to hit posts called a wicket, while a batsman tries to prevent the hit. Cricket is a game that originated in ancient times and developed over the centuries. Organized matches began in the 1700s. Many aspects of baseball are based on the game of cricket. Get a book from the library on cricket. In what ways is it similar to baseball? In what ways is it different?

GLOSSARY

arc—A curved line, as in part of an ellipse or circle.

batting average—A statistic that represents the number of hits divided by the number of times at bat.

elasticity—In physics, the ability of an object to return to its original shape when forced out of shape. A rubber band and a spring are examples of highly elastic objects.

friction—The resistance to motion when two objects rub against each other. Rubbing your hands together on a cold day warms them due to friction. Oil is often used in cars and on certain parts of machinery to reduce friction between moving parts.

fulcrum—The point of support on which a lever turns when moving. The supporting bar on a seesaw is the fulcrum.

gravity (in relation to Earth)—The force with which Earth pulls on an object. The direction of the force is downward toward Earth's center.

hypothesis—A statement based on an educated guess, which can then be proven or disproven by scientific experimentation.

inertia—The resistance of an object to being moved, or if it is already moving, to change its motion.

kinetic energy—The energy that an object has as it is moving; the energy of motion.

mass—The amount of "stuff" that makes up an object.

potential energy—The energy an object has the ability to release.

sample size—A small part of a group that can be inspected to get an idea of the characteristics of the whole group.

scientific method—The step-by-step process scientists take to test whether a hypothesis is true or not.

topping (the ball)—In baseball, hitting a ball above the center of the ball.

torque—A force that causes rotational motion in an object.

transfer of energy—In physics, energy in one object being imparted to another object. For example, if a rolling billiard ball collides with a stationary billiard ball (one sitting at rest), some of the energy of motion in the moving ball will be moved or "transferred" to the stationary ball, causing it to begin to roll.

traction—The amount of friction between an object and the surface across which it is moving.

vector—In physics, a line drawn to indicate the magnitude (amount) and direction of a force, a velocity, or any other quantity that depends on direction.

velocity—Speed; rate of motion over time.

weight—A measure of an object based on the force of gravity on that object.

FURTHER READING

Bochinski, Julianne Blair. ***The Complete Handbook of Science Fair Projects***. Hoboken, N.J.: John Wiley, 2004.

Cook, Sally, and James Charlton. ***Hey Batta Batta Swing!: The Wild Old Days of Baseball***. New York: Simon & Schuster, 2007.

Fitzgerald, Ron. ***Baseball: Becoming A Great Hitter***. Topeka, Kansas: Tandem Library Books, 2000.

Levine, Shar, and Leslie Johnstone. ***Sports Science***. New York: Sterling Publishing Co., 2006.

Mercer, Bobby. ***The Leaping, Sliding, Sprinting, Riding Science Book: 50 Super Sports Science Activities***. New York: Lark Books, 2006.

Ripken, Cal Jr., Bill Ripken, and Larry Burke. ***Play Baseball the Ripken Way: The Complete Illustrated Guide to the Fundamentals***. New York: Ballantine Books, 2005.

Thomas, Keltie. ***How Baseball Works***. Toronto: Maple Tree Press, 2004.

Wiese, Jim. ***Sports Science: 40 Goal-scoring, High-flying, Medal-winning Experiments for Kids***. New York: John Wiley, 2002.

INTERNET ADDRESSES

MLB.com: Kids' Dugout.
<http://www.mlb.com/mlb/
kids/>

Science of Baseball.
<http://www.exploratorium.
edu/baseball/>

USA Softball.
<http://www.usasoftball.
com>

INDEX

ABOUT THE AUTHORS

Robert L. Bonnet has a master's degree in environmental education and has been teaching science for over thirty years. He has organized and judged local and regional science fairs. Dan Keen has a degree in electronic technology. He is the editor and publisher of a county newspaper in southern New Jersey. Together Mr. Bonnet and Mr. Keen have published many science articles and books.